ask uncle jack

100 Years of Wisdom

Uncle Jack & Damon Vonn

Genius Cat Books

Uncle Jack and Damon would like to dedicate this book to the loving memory of Grover, Beth & Junior Van Nordheim.

Special thanks to:

Ozomatli, Karen Kilpatrick & Genius Cat Books, Jeff "Chef" Dean, Richard "Papa" & Monica "Mama" Brinser, Lauren Kerstein, Sandi Israel, Germán Blanco, Joanna "Jo" Austin, Alexis Latshaw, Heather & The Thousand Oaks Mail Center on Avenida De Los Arboles, Claudio, Jackie, and Niko Gutierrez, Sierra Highway and Beale's Cut, Buenos Aires, Argentina, Shirley Temple, Les Paul & Mary Ford, Trio Tariacuri, Hershey's Special Dark Chocolate, Mother Nature, "Silverback" Blue Belly Lizards, and YOU!

www.geniuscatbooks.com

Parkland, FL

ABOUT THIS BOOK

The art for the book was created with pencil and paper and edited with Photoshop. The text was set in Karvwood, Felt Tip Roman, Poppins and Ask Uncle Jack fonts. It was designed by Damon Vonn. Cover, layout, and additional design by Germán Blanco. Text copyright © 2023 by Damon Vonn and Uncle Jack. Illustrations copyright © 2023 by Uncle Jack, Beth Van Nordheim, and Damon Vonn. Colorization by Sandi Israel. Additional editing by Alexis Latshaw. All rights reserved. No part of this publication may be reproduced or distributed in any form or by any means without prior written consent from publisher.
Library of Congress Control Number: 2023938101
ISBN: 978-1-938447-89-1 (hardcover)
First edition, 2023
Our books may be purchased in bulk for promotional, educational, or business use. For more information, or to schedule an event, please visit www.geniuscatbooks.com.
Printed and bound in China.

Our Story

Hello, friends, and welcome!

Uncle Jack and I are overjoyed at the thought of you sitting there, right now, reading these words and holding the book that the two of us dreamt up and brought to life. This book is a testament to the deep bond we share, transcending age and time, and it is with immense gratitude and excitement that we invite you to join us on this literary adventure.

The journey you are about to take is one hundred years in the making. Each page shares wisdom that can only be earned through the passage of time, careful observation of Mother Nature, and a sense of wonder at all that life has to offer. The art throughout the book is a collage of Uncle Jack's sketches and drawings spanning seventy years of his imaginative and eclectic work.

In addition, the process of creating our book was infused with its own special, creative magic. While rummaging through some of Uncle Jack's old boxes, I stumbled upon a precious find: a book of paintings by Jack's mother, Beth (B.V.N.). With Uncle Jack's enthusiastic approval, we made the decision to include two of Beth's colorful and captivating works, as well. Furthermore, this experience of collaborating with Uncle Jack reignited my passion for drawing, reminiscent of when he first taught me the art of sketching. Drawing inspiration from his guidance, I added a few finishing touches and sketches of my own, all of which earned Uncle Jack's resounding endorsement.

You see, Uncle Jack actually IS my granduncle. That's right! We are genuine blood relatives. Uncle Jack, my grandfather's "little" brother, was fifty-five years old when I was born. By then, he had already lived a life filled with extraordinary experiences. He had witnessed the likes of Schlitzie the Pinhead and The Man Who Turned to Stone at the Los Angeles County Fair. It was there that he met an Indian elephant for the first time—a moment from his childhood that he often reminisces about as one that "showed him the true beauty and wonder of nature and changed his life forever."

By the time I entered the world, Uncle Jack had already cultivated his very own "backyard zoo" (as he called it) with raccoons, possums, hawks, pigeons, owls, bobcat kittens, a pet coyote named Tito, and even a Rhesus monkey he talked a neighbor into trading him for an Indian blanket.

Uncle Jack had already snuck a smoke in a hanging lifeboat "to get away," over the side of an Army ship traveling through the Panama Canal, slowly making its fateful way to Australia during World War II.

He had bid farewell to the love of his life in Queensland and continued his service in the New Baggio Province, Philippines. Uncle Jack had already returned home to Glendale, California, and witnessed significant historical events such as the Great Depression, the Cuban Missile Crisis, the assassinations of JFK and MLK, the Vietnam War, and even the moon landing.

His beloved father had already passed—one of his most difficult memories to recall. Uncle Jack has always said, "Taking care of Momma wasn't easy, you know. Daddy was her everything." And by then Uncle Jack had already roamed the coastlines of Morro Bay and Pismo Beach, searching for the perfect log to carve into a mask, while hunting for Native American arrowheads to add to his one-of-a-kind collection.

Truth is, Uncle Jack had already lived an entire lifetime before I'd even tasted my first bite of dark chocolate, and he had already drawn most of the pictures you are about to see. As I reflect on it now, he had indeed already acquired much of the wisdom that fills the pages of this book. And he only needed to spend the next forty-four years graciously sharing and teaching it all to me—a gift that I will treasure forever.

In my infant years, our family was small and very close. We celebrated most holidays and birthdays together, and my earliest memories of Uncle Jack are not of seeing him but rather of hearing and smelling him: his wise, almost cartoon-like tone; his singing and reciting of songs, riddles, poems, and old radio commercials from long ago; and the timeless fragrance of the small bushels of California Black Sage he always carried with him to "keep the evil spirits away." These memories all flood my senses when I think back to the young me and my first curious encounters with my whimsical Uncle Jack.

I was about nine years old when Uncle Jack and I really became close. My parents had separated years before and during the "weeks with Dad" I was mostly alone on a neighborless, ranch-like property up in the hills of Sylmar, fifty miles north of Los Angeles. Uncle Jack's dusty green pinto would come bouncing and squeaking down the driveway and, as he popped the hatchback, I'd run outside, excited to see what new animal or birdhouse or rare treasure might be revealed.

We'd spend endless summer days hiking and exploring the miles and miles of trails on and around the property, catching lizards and snakes, singing songs, sketching and drawing, raising pigeons, and appreciating Mother Nature and all her wonder. We were self-declared "naturalists" and I know in my heart of hearts that those Uncle Jack-guided, magical summer adventures helped make me the person that I am now.

This book is my opportunity to honor and celebrate a man who has inspired me my whole life—not only through his teachings, but through his caring example. And this book is Uncle Jack's opportunity to share one hundred years of carefully cultivated life lessons with you.

We are humbly honored you are here. We hope that this book will inspire you to connect with nature and appreciate the little things. Each page is a tribute to a life well lived and a reminder that we can all learn from the wisdom of those who came before us. We sincerely hope you will find wonder, love, and words to live by and share for the rest of your days.

May you live a long and fulfilling life rich with all of the beauty nature has to offer.

This is Damon, signing off.

hello,
my name
is
uncle jack.

today
is my
birthday
and i'm

100

years old.
i do hope you
make it this long.

yes, my friend,
you read it right!
it's been 100 years
since i was born.

it was late
in the evening
on july 31, 1923,
when my parents
brought me home.

i've seen
many suns rise
and many
moons fall.

and
the advice
i share
with you now,
is the most
important
advice
of all.

go
outside.
spend
time
with
nature.

breathe
the fresh air
and
be kind
to your neighbor.

enjoy
the great
outdoors.
leave that pesky
magic mirror
behind.

Close your eyes
and use your ears.

Listen
to all the
interesting creatures
your curious mind
can find.

there is beauty

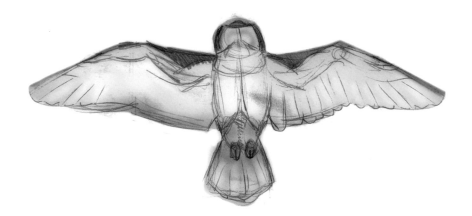

all around us,

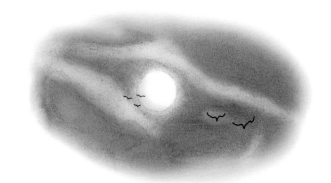

in the vastness
of the sky
and in all
the tiny details
on the ground.

From
the soaring birds
to the crawling insects
— nature offers
endless wonder,

whether you're
looking up
or looking down.

Beth- Sept-1ᵈᵗ 73-

now,
let's go back.
back in time
to 1933.

you see,
growing up
i was different.
being "normal"
wasn't who or what
i could
ever
be.

i was shy
and buck-toothed
and i stuttered...

and
sometimes
other kids
—and even grown-ups—
were rather
mean
to
me.

i often found it hard
to just fit in...

as a boy,
as a teenager,
and as a man.

even...
a very old man.

but hard times,

and difficult people

who did not understand,

helped to make me

the rare person

i am.

And now
you begin to see,
how nature and i
came to be.

when life was
too much,
outside i'd dash,

seeking refuge
under my beloved
live oak tree.

alone

with my thoughts

on a soft bed of grass

and a pillow

made of leaves...

i started to see,
that "me" became "we."

gazing up
through the branches,
at a patch of
blue sky,
my worries
disappeared —

One

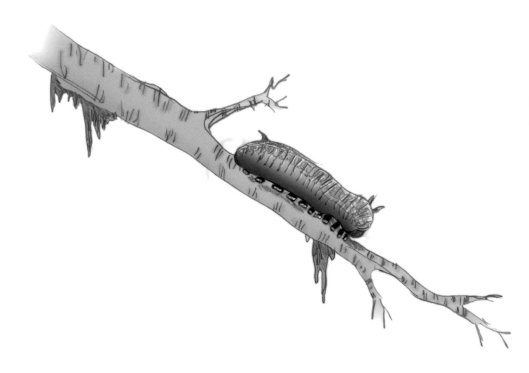

breath

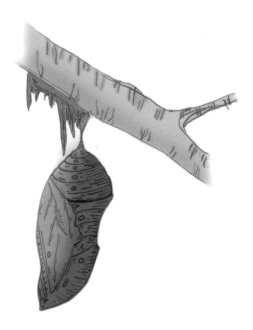

at

time.

well,
that about does it...
that about says it all.

is this where
the story ends?

no!
wait, wait, wait!

Oh my goodness,
there's more!

and maybe
the most important
one yet!

how could
i forget...

dark
chocolate!!!

dark chocolate,
dark chocolate
morning, noon or night...

dark chocolate, dark chocolate
for a long and healthy life!

well
there you go,
now you know.
i have just
a few more things
to share.

A German Pigeon Loft

nune Pigeon

Luben
Pigeon in Dottch

Powder
Pigeon

feather foot.

fantail 9/10/03
UVIII.

60

stay active, friends.

find a hobby you love, and stick with it.

N.G. →

Wire Top + bottom
to tree trunk

Proper Instlation of
Bird house allways
on underside of
trunk or slanting side.
At least 15' up. away
frome wind.

read

reading is the key to wisdom.

Jacks Cabin

Home
Sweet
Home

silent wings of night

sweeten with

honey

instead of sugar.

and
be sure to
appreciate
mother nature,
every day.

68

today is my
birthday
and i'm
100 years old.
i do hope
you make it
this long.

this is uncle jack,
signing off.

Big foot

Stay Curious,
Friends!

Love,
Uncle Jack
&
Damon